C. A. HOLUB

Marseille Provence Travel Guide

Discover top attractions, best restaurants, landmarks, museums, and activities to explore. Find your path.

First published by Pathfinder Travel 2025

Copyright © 2025 by C. A. Holub

All rights reserved. No part of this publication may be reproduced, stored or transmitted in any form or by any means, electronic, mechanical, photocopying, recording, scanning, or otherwise without written permission from the publisher. It is illegal to copy this book, post it to a website, or distribute it by any other means without permission.

C. A. Holub asserts the moral right to be identified as the author of this work.

C. A. Holub has no responsibility for the persistence or accuracy of URLs for external or third-party Internet Websites referred to in this publication and does not guarantee that any content on such Websites is, or will remain, accurate or appropriate.

Designations used by companies to distinguish their products are often claimed as trademarks. All brand names and product names used in this book and on its cover are trade names, service marks, trademarks and registered trademarks of their respective owners. The publishers and the book are not associated with any product or vendor mentioned in this book. None of the companies referenced within the book have endorsed the book.

First edition

This book was professionally typeset on Reedsy.
Find out more at reedsy.com

I would like to dedicate this book to my sister, Debbie. She has always been there for me and is my traveling companion when we journey on vacations together. Thank you for instilling in me the love for travel!

I also dedicate this book to my daughter, Marcy. As time allows, she travels with me as well. We especially like to embark on cruises to our destinations. Thank for sharing these fun times!

Contents

Introduction	1
Pre-Trip Planning and Expectations	3
Getting Settled for Your Stay	10
Wildlife to Expect	14
Top 10 Restaurants and Foods to Eat	18
Top 10 Hikes	32
Best Beaches	38
Top 3 Family Activities	41
Museums to Visit	45
Activities for Adventure Seekers	50
Day Trips	56
Sample 5-Day Itinerary	65
Conclusion	70
Resources	71

Introduction

Welcome to Pathfinder Travel! My name is Carol Holub, and I'm thrilled to write about Marseille in Provence. Traveling is a passion of mine, and it serves as the inspiration behind this book. While this is my first travel guide, I'm excited to soon create a complementary guide about Nice, located in the beautiful French Riviera on France's southern coast.

As I write this travel guide, I'm writing it as if I'd be planning a vacation for myself. The subjects I will be composing are areas I feel are most important when preparing an international trip. From start to finish, I expect to make this travel guide knowledgeable, interesting, and very enjoyable to read. I hope you will be able to see yourself in Marseille as you journey through the guide. Picture you and your loved ones enjoying the parks, recreation, and the wildlife adventures Marseille has to offer. Imagine you are swimming with the dolphins or viewing some of the most beautiful and diverse landscapes while hiking on one of the trails. In this book, my goal is for you to discover exciting adventures as well as seeing the beautiful landscapes of the country and what the south side has to offer you, enhancing your vacation experience.

This handbook is a condensed, easy-to-use travel guide containing information on prices from hotels to flights and from dining to activity costs. You can carry it along with you for the day and check out the *Contents* page for a quick reference. The book aims to bring you pertinent information about Marseille and the journey there, including the top restaurants to dine and recommended dishes. It also brings you the best places for hiking, cycling, and rollerblading. The guide suggests several ideas for adventure or thrill seekers, as well as family-oriented activities. In Marseille, there is something for everyone.

Welcome to Marseille, the second-largest city in France and one of France's most iconic Mediterranean cities, offering a unique blend of history, culture, and breathtaking scenery. Situated along the southern coast of France, Marseille provides an unforgettable experience with stunning coastlines, historical landmarks and architecture, world-class cuisine, and plenty of adventure. It is known for its vibrant port, a strong maritime heritage, and proximity to beautiful natural landscapes.

Expect to be dazzled by the colors of the Mediterranean, surrounded by a mix of traditional and modern French culture. Whether you are looking to relax on the beaches, hike in the hills, or savor some of the best food in the world, Marseille has much to offer.

This guide strives to bring Marseille to life for you. With that being said, let's get started!

Pre-Trip Planning and Expectations

Booking Your Flight

Flight booking should be done well in advance. At least 6 months ahead is preferable. If you are on a tight budget, this will give you the opportunity to pay for your flight before your other trip expenses accumulate.

You may already have a favorite site to book your flight and an airline you prefer to use. If you don't know where to start, I would suggest using www.skyscanner.com, www.kayak.com, www.Expedia.com, or www.booking.com. There is a lot more to choose from, but these are the best in my opinion. The main airlines offering flights to Marseille from the US are American Airlines, United Airlines, Delta, and Air France. Flight prices vary with the departure city and time of booking. The average flight cost is $502-$858 per person.

These sites can help you find the best prices for your trip to Marseille, whether you're looking for flights, accommodations, car rentals, or all three. Each platform has its unique features, so it's a good idea to check multiple options to get the best deals. You may also save money by booking your flight and hotel together. Including your car rental with your flight booking is also an option with many sites. It may be that you prefer using a travel agency for these services. This is more personable, but not as convenient. However, it may be better for you, especially if it's your first time for international travel.

Best Places to Stay

Vieux-Port (Old Port): A central location with easy access to shops, restaurants, and main attractions like the Château d'If and the Notre-Dame de la Garde.

- Hotel: InterContinental Marseille - Hotel Dieu: A 5-star hotel with stunning views, outdoor pool, and fine dining. Price per Night: $235–$375 (€220–€350)
- Hotel: Hôtel La Résidence du Vieux-Port: Charming hotel with views of the Old Port and Notre-Dame de la Garde basilica. Price per Night: $160–$270 (€150–€250)
- Hotel: Sofitel Marseille Vieux-Port: A 5-star property with views of the harbor, rooftop pool, and luxury services. Price per Night: $193–$310 (€180–€290)

Le Panier: The historic district with vibrant street art, quaint cafes, and artisan shops.

- Hotel: Mama Shelter Marseille: Trendy and budget-friendly hotel in the heart of Le Panier with a rooftop bar. Price per Night: $107–$193 (€100–€180)
- Hotel: Hôtel de L'Opéra: Boutique hotel offering vintage decor and a prime location near local markets. Price per Night: $128–$235

(€120–€220)
- Hotel: Hotel Edmond Rostand: Cozy and budget-friendly hotel close to Le Panier with excellent service. Price per Night: $97–$160 (€90–€150)

La Corniche: Offers stunning sea views, with luxury hotels and quiet residential areas.

- Hotel: Radisson Blu Hotel, Marseille Vieux Port: Stylish hotel with sea views, rooftop pool, and modern amenities. Price per Night: $203–$320 (€190–€300)
- Hotel: Hotel Les Bords de Mer: Luxury beachfront hotel with modern design and Mediterranean views. Price per Night: $182–$290 (€170–€270)
- Hotel: Le Provençal: Budget-friendly option with clean rooms and access to local beaches. Price per Night: $107–$160 (€100–€150)

Airbnb

If you prefer more privacy, Airbnb offers a wide range of accommodations in Marseille, catering to various preferences and budgets.

You can find diverse lodging options, including apartments, houses, cottages, and more. The city boasts approximately 17,000 properties, with over 570,000 reviews, indicating a vibrant community of travelers. Family-friendly rentals are abundant, with around 6,100 properties suitable for families. Additionally, pet-friendly accommodations are available, with about 2,800 properties allowing pets. For those seeking amenities like a pool or dedicated workspaces, there are approximately 1,700 properties with a pool and 7,200 with dedicated workspaces. You can find what you need at www.airbnb.com.

Passport

If you already have a passport, that's great! One less thing to do while planning your trip. Make sure that it is not expired or will soon expire while working on everything else! If it is 10 months until expiration while planning your trip, you may want to renew your passport. Most countries require your passport to be valid 6 months after your trip return date. If your passport is set to expire within 6 months of your departure or return, you may be denied entry or boarding. Many airlines will also require that your passport be valid for at least 6 months before boarding an international flight, regardless of the destination's requirements.

If you need a passport, allow 8-11 weeks to receive it after applying. There are several places you can apply for a passport. Many *post offices* can assist you with the passport application process and take your passport photo. Visit the U.S. Postal Service's website at www.usps.com to find a nearby post office that accepts passport applications. You will need to complete the passport application form (DS-11 for new applicants) and schedule an appointment at participating locations. I used the post office to apply for mine. This by far is the best option in my opinion.

Other options: *US Department of State* www.travel.state.gov - You must make an appointment through the U.S. Department of State website to visit a passport agency or center. *Clerk of courts* - check with your local clerk's office for passport acceptance and availability. Visit your county clerk's website for specific information. *Travel agencies* - some travel agencies are authorized to submit passport applications on your behalf. They often offer expedited services for an additional fee.

For new passports, you will typically need the following:

- Completed DS-11 form (available online).
- Proof of U.S. citizenship (e.g., birth certificate, naturalization certificate).
- Proof of identity (e.g., driver's license, government-issued ID).
- Passport photo (2x2 inches).
- Passport fees (varies depending on the type of application and processing speed).

Passport prices (8-11 weeks): $130 for adults, 16 years and older; $100 for minors under age 16. Expedited prices (5-7 weeks): $190 for adults and $160 for minors.

For passport renewals, you can follow the process online (if eligible) at www.travel.state.gov or use the DS-82 form if applying by mail. Prices are the same as getting a new passport.

Currency to Use

France uses the Euro (€). Currency can be exchanged at airports, exchange offices, or ATMs. Most ATMs in France accept international debit and credit cards (Visa, Mastercard) and will dispense Euros when you withdraw cash. ATMs at airports, train stations, and city centers are the best places to find machines that accept international cards. While most establishments in Marseille accept major credit and debit cards, it is always a good idea to have some cash on hand for smaller purchases.

Even though many locations accept USD, it is recommended to use the Euro if purchasing with cash or leaving tips.

Tip: Inform your bank of your travel plans before using your debit card abroad. Getting your purchases approved before your trip may avoid possible purchase delays and embarrassment if transactions are denied. This verification process depends on your bank.

What to Pack

The clothing to pack depends on the time of year. Pack clothes according to Marseille's weather. I always make a list of things to take and mark them off when they are packed. Some things to consider other than clothing: comfortable walking shoes, toiletries, wallet including money, credit and debit cards, and driver's license; passport, medications, medical information, swimsuit and accessories, sunglasses, sunscreen, camera, laptop, phone, all chargers. This is a start. Add on where needed.

Airport

You will be arriving at Marseille Provence Airport (MRS). It is the main international airport serving Marseille and the Provence region. Located about 17 miles (27 km) northwest of Marseille, it offers both domestic and international flights to major European and global

PRE-TRIP PLANNING AND EXPECTATIONS

destinations. The airport has two terminals, one for full-service airlines and another for low-cost carriers. It provides transport options like buses, taxis, rental cars, and a shuttle to the train station for easy access to the city.

Tips: Marseille has excellent public transport systems (trains, trams, buses), but renting a car is a great option if you plan to explore the surrounding areas, like the Calanques National Park or nearby towns along the coast of Provence. If you chose to rent a car through your flight booking online or through your travel agency, your reservation will be at the car rental service desk in which you reserved your car. The car rental center is located in Terminal 1.

Getting Settled for Your Stay

Car Rental

Renting a car in Marseille is a popular and convenient option for exploring France south side and its surrounding areas. Located in Terminal 1, Marseille Provence Airport (MRS) has a wide range of car rental agencies offering various vehicle types to suit different budgets. Consider renting a compact vehicle for easy navigation, especially if you plan to visit scenic or rural areas with narrow roads. Keep in mind that Marseille can have heavy traffic, especially in the summer months, and parking can be limited in tourist-heavy areas. Here is a detailed breakdown of rental car options at Marseille Provence Airport (MRS), including price ranges.

Car Rental Agencies at Marseille Provence Airport (MRS) include Europcar, Avis, Hertz, Sixt, Enterprise, Budget, and Thrifty.

Car Rental Choices & Price Ranges (per day):

The price of a rental car can vary based on the type of car, the rental period, and the season. Here are some common categories and price estimates.

GETTING SETTLED FOR YOUR STAY

- Economy cars such as the Fiat 500, Renault Clio, and Peugeot 208 price range is $32–$75 (€30–€70) per day.
- Compact cars such as the Opel Astra, Ford Focus, and Toyota Yaris price range is $53–$96 (€50–€90) per day.
- Luxury & Premium cars like the BMW 3 Series, Mercedes-Benz C-Class price range $128–$267 (€120–€250) per day.
- SUVs & 4x4s such as the Nissan Qashqai, Peugeot 3008, Range Rover Evoque price range is $75–$171 (€70–€160) per day.
- Minivans & MPVs such as the Renault Espace, Volkswagen Sharan price range is $107–$214 (€100–€200) per day.
- Convertible Sports Cars like the Audi A3 Cabriolet, BMW Z4 price range is $160–$320 (€150–€300) per day.

Price Factors

- Season: Prices will be higher during peak tourist seasons (spring and summer) and lower in the off-season (autumn and winter).
- Duration: Longer rentals often offer better daily rates.
- Insurance: Basic insurance is included in most rentals, but you may wish to add extra coverage for peace of mind.

Tips for Renting a Car

Booking in Advance: It's often cheaper to book your rental car in advance, especially if you're traveling during the busy summer months. You may want to book your car rental at the time you book your flight and hotel.

- Driver's License: You'll need a valid driver's license to rent a car. Non-EU visitors may need an International Driver's Permit (IDP).
- Fuel: Make sure to return the car with a full tank of fuel to avoid extra charges.
- Traffic and Parking: Both cities have narrow streets and limited parking, especially in the Old Town (Vieux-Nice and Le Panier). It's a good idea to research parking options in advance.
- Road Tolls: The French highways (autoroutes) have tolls, so be prepared to pay toll fees if you plan to drive long distances along the coast or to nearby cities.

Car rental in Marseille Provence Airport (MRS) offers a wide range of options to suit every traveler's needs and budget. Whether you're looking for an affordable economy car, a spacious SUV, or a luxury convertible to cruise along the Riviera, you'll find plenty of choices. Be sure to book in advance, especially during peak tourist seasons, and enjoy the freedom of exploring the stunning landscapes of southern France!

Local Supermarkets and Grocery Stores

If you need to budget more on your trip, you may think about purchasing food at a local market. Though you want to experience the Mediterranean cuisine, dining out for every meal can be quite expensive. Here are some markets you may want to consider.

Carrefour and **Intermarché** are the most common supermarket chains in the city, where you can find local products like fresh bread, cheeses, and wines.

GETTING SETTLED FOR YOUR STAY

Marché de la Plaine: A lively open-air market offering fresh fruits, vegetables, and local delicacies.

Wildlife to Expect

The wildlife around Marseille is incredibly diverse, with a mix of terrestrial and marine species that reflect the unique geography and climate of Provence. The city is surrounded by natural parks and coastal regions, making them prime spots for nature lovers and wildlife enthusiasts.

Being close to the Mediterranean coast, Marseille has a thriving marine ecosystem. If you're into wildlife watching, consider visiting Calanques National Park for a chance to spot Mediterranean sea life, such as dolphins, sea turtles, and various bird species like the Bonelli's eagle.

Calanques National Park

The Calanques are rocky inlets along the Mediterranean coast, forming part of a protected national park. They are known for their breathtaking landscapes, steep cliffs, turquoise waters, and rich biodiversity.

WILDLIFE TO EXPECT

Terrestrial Wildlife includes wild boar, goats, foxes and small mammals, birdlife such as such as the Mediterranean gull and peregrine falcon, and the Audouin's Gull, a rare species that breeds in the Calanques.

Audouin's Gull

The crystal-clear waters around the Calanques are home to an incredible range of marine species, making it a popular spot for divers and snorkelers.

Marine Life consists of fish species like groupers, octopuses, sea bass, and goby fish in the waters. Common dolphins are often seen off the coast. Sperm whales and blue whales can be spotted in deeper waters. Mediterranean monk seals were once present in the area and are occasionally sighted.

The park also supports unique flora such as lavender, thyme, and rosemary, which attract various insect species. Cistus and oak trees are also common in the landscape.

Urban Parks

In addition to the natural parks, Marseille's urban parks also provide habitats for wildlife. Parc Borely is home to various bird species, including ducks and pigeons. Parc National des Calanques is a protected area that provides sanctuary to a mix of rare plants and animals.

Top 10 Restaurants and Foods to Eat

Le Petit Nice Passedat: A Michelin-starred restaurant offering seafood with incredible views of the Mediterranean.

Recommended Dishes:

Bouillabaisse (Traditional Fish Stew): A signature dish of Marseille, this traditional fish stew comes with a variety of local fish, shellfish, and a flavorful broth. Price: $70 (€65)

Lobster with Saffron Sauce: Fresh Mediterranean lobster served with a rich, aromatic saffron sauce, beautifully balanced in flavor. Price: $80 (€75)

Mediterranean Sea Bream with Vegetables: A delicate, perfectly cooked Mediterranean sea bream served with fresh seasonal vegetables and a citrusy dressing. Price: $53 (€50)

Chez Fonfon: Known for its bouillabaisse (traditional fish stew), a quintessential Marseille dish.

Recommended Dishes:

Bouillabaisse: A famous traditional fish stew made with local fish, shellfish, and herbs, served with garlic rouille sauce. Price: $59 (€55)

Fried Calamari: Lightly fried calamari served with lemon and aioli. Price: $19 (€18)

Pan-Seared Sea Bass: Perfectly seared Mediterranean sea bass with a side of roasted vegetables. Price: $23 (€22)

La Table de l'Olivier: French Mediterranean cuisine in a charming setting.

Recommended Dishes:

Seafood Risotto: Creamy risotto with mussels, shrimp, and calamari. Price: $24 (€22)

Tuna Tartare with Avocado: Fresh tuna mixed with creamy avocado and topped with a light citrus dressing. Price: $19 (€18)

Lemon and Olive Oil Cake: A fragrant and light cake made with fresh lemons and Mediterranean olive oil. Price: $10 (€9)

Le Miramar: Located on the Old Port, serving high-quality seafood with amazing views.

Recommended Dishes:

Bouillabaisse: A flavorful Marseille fish stew made with local seafood, herbs, and served with a variety of accompaniments. Price: $64 (€60)

Grilled Lobster: Fresh lobster grilled to perfection and served with garlic butter. Price: $48 (€45)

Tarte Tatin: A caramelized apple tart served warm with a scoop of vanilla ice cream. Price: $11 (€10)

L'Épuisette: A Michelin-starred spot with stunning views and exquisite seafood.

Recommended Dishes:

Bouillabaisse: The classic Marseille dish of fish stew, prepared with a variety of Mediterranean seafood. Price: $75 (€70)

Seafood Platter: A selection of fresh oysters, shrimp, mussels, and other Mediterranean seafood. Price: $64 (€60)

Profiteroles with Chocolate Sauce: A light, crisp pastry filled with vanilla ice cream and topped with rich chocolate sauce. Price: $13 (€12)

Les Trois Forts: Located on the top floor of the Sofitel, offering a panoramic view and sophisticated French dishes.

Recommended Dishes:

Tuna Tartare with Wasabi and Cucumber: Fresh tuna mixed with cucumber and seasoned with a hint of wasabi for an extra kick. Price: $24 (€22)

Grilled Mediterranean Sea Bass: A perfectly grilled Mediterranean sea bass served with vegetables and citrus dressing. Price: $34 (€32)

Chocolate Soufflé: A warm, gooey chocolate soufflé served with a scoop of vanilla ice cream. Price: $15 (€14)

Le Café des Épices: An innovative bistro blending Mediterranean ingredients with modern cooking.

Recommended Dishes:

Mediterranean Mezze Platter: A platter of assorted Mediterranean tapas including hummus, falafel, and grilled vegetables. Price: $24 (€22)

Duck Breast with Orange Sauce: A tender duck breast, perfectly cooked and complemented with a tangy orange sauce. Price: $31 (€29)

Lemon and Almond Cake: A sweet, zesty cake with a delicate almond flavor. Price: $10 (€9)

L'Alcove: A contemporary bistro with a focus on seasonal ingredients and Mediterranean flavors.

Recommended Dishes:

Marinated Octopus Salad with Lemon and Olive Oil: A fresh, light salad with marinated octopus, zesty lemon, and extra virgin olive oil. Price: $19 (€18)

Roasted Lamb Shoulder with Rosemary: Slow-cooked, tender lamb shoulder paired with rosemary and seasonal vegetables. Price: $30 (€28)

Pistachio Cake with Raspberry Coulis: A delicious, moist pistachio cake with tangy raspberry coulis. Price: $11 (€10)

La Brasserie des Capitolaux: Offering traditional French brasserie cuisine, this restaurant specializes in hearty meals and excellent wines.

Recommended Dishes:

Escargots de Bourgogne: French escargots cooked in garlic butter, a classic French delicacy. Price: $16 (€15)

Steak Frites: A juicy, tender steak served with crispy French fries. Price: $30 (€28)

Crème Brûlée: A creamy, rich vanilla crème brûlée with a caramelized sugar crust. Price: $10 (€9)

TOP 10 RESTAURANTS AND FOODS TO EAT

Le Passage: A contemporary restaurant with a modern take on classic French cuisine.

Recommended Dishes:

Foie Gras with Fig Jam: A smooth foie gras served with a sweet fig jam, creating a perfect balance of flavors. Price: $34 (€32)

Duck Confit with Garlic Potatoes: Slow-cooked duck leg served with crispy garlic potatoes. Price: $30 (€28)

Tarte Tatin: A delicious, warm caramelized apple tart served with vanilla ice cream. Price: $10 (€9)

TOP 10 RESTAURANTS AND FOODS TO EAT

The prices reflect mid-range to high-end dining options in Marseille, showcasing a range of local specialties, Mediterranean ingredients, and classic French dishes. These prices can fluctuate based on the season, day of the week, and restaurant popularity, so it's always good to check the current menu when planning your visit.

I hope this guide helps you navigate the top culinary spots in Marseille, with a variety of excellent dishes to try at each restaurant! Enjoy your culinary adventure!

Top 10 Hikes

These hikes provide a perfect mix of landscapes, from coastal cliffs to lush valleys, allowing you to experience the incredible natural beauty of the 10 most popular trails, including Calanques National Park and Cap Canaille. Each trail offers different levels of difficulty, so there's something for every kind of hiker, from beginners to seasoned adventurers. Enjoy your hike!

Calanques National Park – Sormiou to Morgiou: One of the most famous hikes in Marseille, offering incredible views of the rugged coastline, limestone cliffs, and turquoise Mediterranean waters. The hike is moderately difficult to walk. It is 6.2 miles (10 km) in length and takes 4-6 hours to complete.

TOP 10 HIKES

Cap Canaille – Cassis: This hike takes you along the impressive Cap Canaille, which is one of the highest sea cliffs in France, offering spectacular panoramic views over the Cassis coastline. Hiking is moderately difficult. It is 5.6 miles (9 km) long, with a duration of 3-4 hours.

Calanques de Sugiton: A short but rewarding hike through one of the most famous calanques, Sugiton which presents a variety of landscapes along the trail. This hike is moderately difficult, is 5 miles (8 km) in length, and takes 3-4 hours to conclude.

The Grotte Cosquer Trail: An ancient cave with prehistoric paintings. This is a scenic hike for those interested in history and adventure. The hike is moderate to difficult, is 4.3 miles (7 km) long, with 3-4 hours duration.

Notre-Dame de la Garde to the Calanques: This hike offers great views over the city of Marseille and the surrounding coastline. It's an excellent choice for those who want a shorter hike that still offers spectacular views. Hike is moderately difficult, is 3.7 miles (6 km) long, and takes 2-3 hours for completion.

Mont Puget: The hike is challenging, but the reward is breathtaking. The route is rugged, with some rocky sections, so it's best suited for experienced hikers. This is a difficult hike, which is 7.5 miles (12 km), with a duration of 5-6 hours.

Parc National des Calanques: Port-Miou to En-Vau: This trail takes you from Port-Miou to En-Vau, two of the most beautiful calanques in the region. The hike offers diverse landscapes, and dramatic views of the Mediterranean. The hike is moderately difficult, and is 5 miles (8 km) long, taking 4-5 hours to finish.

The Ridge Trail – Calanque de Sugiton to Calanque de Morgiou: This is a demanding hike along the ridge between two of the most famous calanques. It's a great hike for experienced hikers who want to challenge themselves with elevation changes and rocky paths while soaking in the incredible landscape. This hike is difficult, being 6.2 miles (10 km) in length, and taking 5-6 hours to complete.

Mont Saint-Hilaire: This hike offers great panoramic views over the coastline of Marseille. The hike is perfect for those looking to explore the surrounding countryside with a view. It's moderately difficult, is 4.3 miles (7 km) in length, and takes 3-4 hours to achieve.

Calanque de Sormiou to Sugiton: A beautiful coastal trail that takes you from Sormiou, one of the largest calanques, to Sugiton. You'll enjoy stunning coastal views along the way, with plenty of opportunities for a swim in the crystal-clear waters at the end. This trail is moderately difficult, and is 3.7 miles (6 km) long, with 3-4 hours duration.

Best Beaches

Plage du Prado – One of Marseille's largest and most popular beaches, great for families and water sports. It has a mix of sand and pebbles, plus facilities like restaurants and volleyball courts. The beach is easily accessible by public transport, making it a convenient spot for both locals and tourists. With lifeguards on duty during peak seasons, it's a safe and enjoyable destination for swimmers of all ages.

Plage des Catalans – A small, sandy beach close to the city center, perfect for a quick swim with a lively atmosphere. It's popular among locals and has volleyball courts and nearby cafés. Due to its central location, it can get quite crowded, especially in the summer months. The beach offers stunning views of the Mediterranean, making it a great spot to relax and enjoy the sunset.

Calanque de Sugiton – A stunning cove in Calanques National Park, with crystal-clear waters and dramatic limestone cliffs. It requires a moderate hike to reach but offers a breathtaking, secluded beach experience. The hike to the cove rewards visitors with panoramic views of the Mediterranean, making it a favorite among nature lovers and photographers. Due to its remote location, the waters remain pristine, perfect for snorkeling and exploring marine life.

Plage de la Pointe Rouge – One of Marseille's largest sandy beaches, popular for kayaking, windsurfing, and paddleboarding. It has a relaxed vibe and plenty of beachfront restaurants. The shallow waters make it ideal for families with young children looking for a safe place to swim. In the evenings, the beachside restaurants and bars create a lively yet laid-back atmosphere perfect for unwinding by the sea.

Plage de l'Huveaune – A quieter extension of Plage du Prado, with soft sand and shallow waters, making it ideal for families and sunbathers. Its peaceful ambiance makes it a great spot for those looking to escape the crowds while still enjoying the convenience of nearby facilities. The gentle waves also make it a favorite for beginner swimmers and those looking to relax in the water.

Anse de Malmousque – A hidden rocky cove near Vallon des Auffes, perfect for swimming and snorkeling in clear waters. It's not a traditional sandy beach but offers a peaceful escape. With its rugged charm and fewer crowds, it's a favorite spot for locals seeking a quiet retreat by the sea. The surrounding rocks provide great sunbathing spots, while the calm waters make it ideal for a refreshing dip.

Calanque de Morgiou – A breathtaking cove in Calanques National Park, surrounded by towering cliffs and turquoise waters. Accessible by hiking or boating, it's a serene spot for swimming and exploring nature. The small fishing port within the calanque adds to its charm, offering a glimpse of the area's maritime history. Its rich marine life also makes it a great spot for snorkeling and discovering underwater beauty.

Top 3 Family Activities

Visit **Parc Borély**, a beautiful park with a lake and playgrounds. One of the city's most beloved green spaces offering a serene escape from the hustle and bustle of the urban environment. It combines natural beauty, historical architecture, and recreational opportunities, making it a popular destination for both locals and visitors. Parc Borély is one of Marseille's hidden gems, offering a perfect mix of history, nature, and recreation. Whether you're looking for a relaxing day in the park, a visit to a museum, or a place to enjoy outdoor sports, Parc Borély has something for everyone. Its stunning gardens, serene atmosphere, and cultural offerings make it a must-visit location in Marseille.

Explore the **MuCEM** (Museum of European and Mediterranean Civilizations) for an interactive cultural experience. The MuCEM is one of Marseille's most renowned and modern museums, showcasing the diverse history and cultures of the Mediterranean region. Its striking architecture, featuring a sleek lattice design, offers stunning views of the Old Port and the sea. Inside, visitors can explore a mix of permanent and temporary exhibitions, covering topics from ancient civilizations to contemporary social issues. The museum also connects to Fort Saint-Jean via a scenic footbridge, allowing for a seamless blend of history and modernity.

Go on a boat trip to the **Calanques**, perfect for families to see wildlife and enjoy the sea. One of the best ways to experience the stunning beauty of the region. The Calanques National Park is renowned for its dramatic cliffs, crystal-clear waters, and hidden coves, and a boat trip offers a unique vantage point of this natural wonder. There are half-day tours and full-day tours to consider.

Half-day tours, 3-4 hours: price - $43-$65 (€40 to €60) per person, offer an excellent introduction to the Calanques. Sightseeing, photo opportunities, and the chance to swim in secluded coves are available.

Full-day tours, 6-8 hours: price - $82-$130 (€75 to €120) per person, offer a more in-depth exploration of the Calanques. These tours may include stops at several Calanques and sometimes even the nearby islands. Highlights for this tour include extended exploration, swimming, sightseeing, and often lunch. Private boat tours are also available.

A boat trip to the Calanques is an unforgettable way to experience the stunning natural beauty of Marseille's coastline. Whether you're looking for a quick half-day excursion, a full-day adventure, or a private, intimate boat ride, there are plenty of options to choose from. Prices vary depending on the type of tour and duration, but the experience is well worth the cost, offering breathtaking views, opportunities for swimming and relaxation, and a glimpse into the rich biodiversity of this remarkable region.

Museums to Visit

These museums provide a rich experience of the history, art, and culture of Marseille, with a blend of modern and traditional art, as well as fascinating insights into the local heritage and Mediterranean connections. The admission prices are standard for most of the museums in Marseille, but they may occasionally change depending on temporary exhibitions or special events. Additionally, most museums offer free admission for certain groups, like children under 18, students (especially EU residents under 26), and during special events like the first Sunday of each month.

MuCEM: Museum of European and Mediterranean Civilizations. The MuCEM is one of Marseille's most renowned and modern museums, showcasing the diverse history and cultures of the Mediterranean region. The exhibits cover a broad range of topics, including anthropology, archaeology, contemporary art, and Mediterranean cultural heritage. The striking architecture of the museum itself, the rooftop terrace with panoramic views over the city and the sea, and the beautiful Fort Saint-Nicolas offering a glimpse into the city's military past are highlights of the museum. Admission is $10 (€9) adults and $7 (€6) students and seniors. Free for those under 26 years old (EU residents), disabled visitors, and on the first Sunday of each month.

Musée d'Histoire de Marseille: Dive deep into the city's ancient roots and maritime history. In-depth look at the rich history of Marseille, from its founding by the Greeks around 600 BC to its development as a major port city and its role in trade, colonization, and immigration. The museum displays a mix of archaeological finds, historical objects, and artifacts that illustrate the city's rise to prominence in the Mediterranean. Highlights include the remains of a Roman shipwreck, ancient mosaics, and the spectacular Vieux-Port (Old Port) view from the museum's upper floors. Admission is $7 (€6) adults and $3 (€3) students and seniors. Free for those under 18 years old, EU residents under 26, and on the first Sunday of each month.

Musée des Beaux-Arts de Marseille (Museum of Fine Arts): This museum, housed in the historic Palais des Beaux-Arts, offers an impressive collection of artwork spanning centuries, including French, Italian, and Dutch masterpieces. It showcases works from the Renaissance to the early 20th century, with particular emphasis on 19th-century French art. The exceptional collection of 19th-century French paintings, sculptures, and beautiful architecture of the museum itself are the highlights. Admission is $7 (€6) adults and $3 (€3) students and seniors. Free for those under 18 years old, EU residents under 26, and on the first Sunday of each month.

Musée d'Archéologie Méditerranéenne (Museum of Mediterranean Archaeology): This museum focuses on the ancient civilizations of the Mediterranean, with a particular emphasis on Greece, Egypt, and Rome. The museum houses important archaeological collections, including Egyptian mummies, Roman artifacts, Greek pottery, and a wealth of objects that illustrate daily life in ancient Mediterranean cultures. It's a must-see for anyone interested in ancient Mediterranean history and archaeology. Admission is $4 (€4) adults and $2 (€2) reduced. Free for those under 18 years old, EU residents under 26, and on the first Sunday of each month.

La Vieille Charité: Located in a historic 17th-century building, La Vieille Charité that houses a collection of temporary art exhibitions, as well as a museum dedicated to the history of the building and its cultural significance in Marseille. It's an excellent spot to learn about Marseille's role as a historical and cultural crossroads. The highlights are the beautiful architecture of the building, the courtyard, and the rooftop

MUSEUMS TO VISIT

offering views of the Old Town, as well as the varied art exhibitions. Admission is $6 (€5) adults and $3 (€3) reduced. Free for those under 18 years old, EU residents under 26, and on the first Sunday of each month.

Activities for Adventure Seekers

Marseille offers adventure seekers the perfect blend of rugged landscapes, dramatic coastlines, and a variety of outdoor sports. Whether you're looking for high-energy pursuits on land or thrilling experiences in the water, the south of France delivers incredible opportunities to explore and push your limits.+

Rock Climbing in Calanques National Park: With its sharp limestone cliffs towering above the Mediterranean, the park offers a variety of routes suitable for both beginners and experienced climbers. Local companies offer guided rock climbing tours, providing all the necessary equipment and ensuring a safe experience. Some popular climbing spots in the Calanques include Sormiou and En-Vau. These areas have some of the best climbing routes in France, and after a climb, you can cool off with a swim in the pristine waters below.

ACTIVITIES FOR ADVENTURE SEEKERS

Guided Climbing Tours: Half-day tours: $55 to $100 (€50 to €90) per person. Full-day tours: $110 to $165 (€100 to €150) per person, depending on the route and guide.

Rental Equipment: If you need equipment, expect to pay around $16 to $33 USD (€15 to €30) per day for a full set (harness, helmet, ropes).

Sea Kayaking and Paddleboarding in Calanques: For a more serene yet adventurous activity, sea kayaking or stand-up paddleboarding (SUP) in the Calanques offers a fantastic way to experience the rugged coastline of Marseille from the water. Best for all skill levels, with options for guided tours for beginners. You'll paddle through the Calanques, stopping at secluded beaches and caves along the way. Guides provide safety instructions, and the activity can be enjoyed at your own pace or as part of a more intense workout.

Kayak Rental: Half-day rental: $22 to $44 (€20 to €40).

Full-day rental: $44 to $66 (€40 to €60).

Tandem kayaks - $44 to $66 USD (€40 to €60) for a half-day.

Stand-up Paddleboard (SUP) Rental:

ACTIVITIES FOR ADVENTURE SEEKERS

Half-day rental: $22 to $44 (€20 to €40).

Full-day rental: $44 to $66 USD (€40 to €60).

Guided Tour: If you prefer guided experience, group kayak tours or SUP tours in the Calanques cost $44 to $66 (€40 to €60) per person for 2-3 hours.

Paragliding over the Mediterranean: For the ultimate adrenaline rush, paragliding in Marseille offers an exciting way to soar above the Mediterranean coastline. With professional pilots guiding you, you'll experience stunning aerial views of the city, the Calanques, and the crystal-clear waters below. Best for all thrill-seekers; no prior experience is required. Launching from L'Estaque or Marseille's hills, you'll enjoy a breathtaking flight with views that span from the city to the horizon. Some packages include tandem flights, where you're accompanied by a certified pilot.

Tandem Paragliding Flight: $110 to $175 (€100 to €160) for a 20 to 30-minute flight, depending on the location (e.g., L'Estaque or Les Goudes).

Longer Flights: $165 to $220 (€150 to €200) for 30 to 45 minutes.

Caving in the Calanques: For those seeking something a bit different, caving in the Calanques provides an exciting challenge.

Explore underground caves and tunnels carved into the limestone rock, with some caves only accessible by climbing or swimming. Best for experienced adventurers or those with a passion for underground exploration. You'll navigate through dark, narrow passages and cavernous chambers, all the while learning about the geology and history of the region. It's an exhilarating activity that requires a head for adventure.

ACTIVITIES FOR ADVENTURE SEEKERS

Guided Caving Tours: Half-day tours: $66 to $110 USD (€60 to €100) per person.

Group Rates: $55 to $88 (€50 to €80) per person, depending on the size of the group and the difficulty of the cave.

Whether you're looking for water sports, aerial views, or challenging physical activities, Marseille offers a wide variety of exciting experiences for adventure seekers. From scaling cliffs in the Calanques to paragliding over the Mediterranean or exploring remote canyons, the city provides an adrenaline-filled escape for those craving excitement in the heart of Provence. Be sure to book in advance, especially during the high season, to ensure availability and get the best prices!

Day Trips

Calanques National Park: The Calanques National Park is one of the most beautiful natural sites in France, featuring rugged limestone cliffs, turquoise waters, and hidden inlets. This protected marine area is a paradise for outdoor enthusiasts, offering hiking, swimming, and boat tours. The park stretches along the Mediterranean coast, from Marseille to Cassis, and it's best known for its dramatic scenery and crystal-clear waters.

Distance: Approximately 30 minutes by car from Marseille

Duration: A full-day trip

Highlights:

- Calanque de Sormiou: A stunning inlet surrounded by cliffs, perfect for a swim or a picnic.

DAY TRIPS

- Calanque d'En-Vau: One of the most famous and isolated calanques, accessible via a challenging hike, offering a serene beach and picturesque views.
- Boat Tours: You can take a boat tour from Marseille or Cassis to visit multiple calanques from the sea, which offers a unique perspective of the cliffs and secluded beaches.

- Hiking Trails: There are various trails for different skill levels, including routes that lead you up to incredible viewpoints overlooking the coastline.
- Swimming & Snorkeling: In the warmer months, you can swim in the calm waters of the calanques, where marine life is abundant.

Best Time to Visit: The best time to visit the Calanques is during spring or early autumn, as the summer months can get hot and crowded. The park is accessible year-round, but you should check the weather conditions, especially during the winter when some paths may be closed due to heavy rainfall or risk of wildfires.

Transportation: You can reach the Calanques by taking a bus from Marseille to various places like Sormiou, Callelongue, or Les Goudes, or rent a car to drive to the park. A boat tour from Cassis or Marseille's Old Port also provides an alternative method of exploration.

What to Bring: Comfortable hiking shoes, sunscreen, water, and swimwear.

Cassis: A charming fishing village located on the Mediterranean coast, just a short drive from Marseille. Known for its picturesque harbor, colorful buildings, and stunning coastline, it's an ideal destination for a relaxing day trip. The village is also famous for its Cassis wine, made from local vineyards, and is surrounded by breathtaking cliffs and beaches.

Distance: 30 to 40 minutes by car from Marseille

Duration: Half-day to full-day trip

Highlights:

- Cassis Harbor: Take a leisurely stroll around the harbor, lined with restaurants, cafés, and colorful boats. It's a perfect spot for a

relaxing lunch overlooking the water.
- Wine Tasting: Cassis is known for its white wines, particularly those made from the local Calanques grape. There are several vineyards around the village where you can sample the wines and learn about the production process.

- Calanques de Cassis: In addition to the national park, Cassis is home to its own calanques. You can take a boat tour or hike along trails to visit these beautiful coves and enjoy secluded beaches.
- Plage de la Grande Mer: A lovely beach close to the village center, perfect for relaxing by the sea.
- Cape Canaille: The highest sea cliff in Europe, offering stunning panoramic views of the Mediterranean coast. You can hike up to the top or take a scenic drive along the cliffside

Best Time to Visit: The best time to visit Cassis is spring and early autumn, as the village is quieter and the weather is perfect for outdoor activities. Summer months can be busy, especially with tourists flocking to the beaches and the vineyards.

Transportation: Cassis is easily accessible from Marseille by car, and you can also take a train to Cassis station followed by a short bus ride to the town center.

What to Bring: Comfortable shoes for walking, sunscreen, a hat, and swimwear if you plan to swim at the beach.

Aix-en-Provence: A beautiful town known for its markets, spas, and lavender fields. It's a stunning town filled with historical charm, artistic heritage, and natural beauty. The town sits at the foot of the Sainte-Victoire Mountain and is known for its natural beauty, warm Mediterranean climate, and rich cultural heritage. It is easily accessible from Marseille, making it an ideal day-trip destination or a base for exploring Provence.

Distance: 30 to 40 minutes by car from Marseille

Duration: Half-day to full-day trip

Highlights:

- Cours Mirabeau: A wide, tree-lined avenue with fountains and cafes, perfect for strolling.
- Saint-Sauveur Cathedral: A beautiful medieval cathedral with an impressive façade and historical significance.
- Place d'Albertas: A charming square surrounded by elegant 17th-century buildings.
- Paul Cézanne's Studio (Atelier Cézanne): Visit the studio where the artist worked on some of his most famous paintings.
- Sainte-Victoire Mountain: Ideal for hiking and offering stunning views of the surrounding region.
- Museums: The Granet Museum, which showcases works by Cézanne, Picasso, and other notable artists.
- Markets: Aix-en-Provence has vibrant farmers and artisan markets, such as the Marché Provençal.

- Thermal Spas: Aix is known for its natural hot springs, with historical baths dating back to Roman times.

Best Time to Visit: The best time to visit Aix-en-Provence is during the spring (April to June) and autumn (September to October) months. During these times, the weather is pleasant with mild temperatures, and the crowds are less than in peak summer.

Summer (July to August) is also popular but can be very hot, with temperatures often rising above 30°C (86°F), and the town can become crowded with tourists.

Winter (December to February) is quieter and cooler, but you can still enjoy the peaceful atmosphere.

Transportation:

Train: The Aix-en-Provence TGV station connects the town to other major cities in France, including Paris and Marseille. From the TGV station, you can take a local bus or taxi to the town center.

Bus: Several regional buses run between Aix and Marseille, as well as other nearby towns.

Car: Renting a car is a good option if you want to explore the surrounding countryside or visit nearby towns like Cassis or Lourmarin.

What to Bring: Comfortable walking shoes, light clothing, hat, sunscreen, camera or sketchbook, water bottle, light jacket or sweater.

Sample 5-Day Itinerary

Arrival Day 1: Getting Settled & Exploring the Old Port

What to do will depend on the time of your arrival. Here is a plan for a leisure day. Adjust according to your time of arrival.

Morning:

- Arrive in Marseille.
- Settle into your accommodation.
- Take a leisurely walk to Vieux-Port (Old Port), the heart of the city.

Afternoon:

- Lunch at Maison Geney - a cozy café offering fresh sandwiches, salads, and pastries - perfect for a light, delicious meal.
- Visit Basilique Notre-Dame de la Garde, perched on a hill with panoramic views of the city and the Mediterranean Sea.
- Explore the Le Panier District, the oldest neighborhood in Marseille, known for its narrow streets, colorful houses, and vibrant art scene.

Evening:

- Dinner at Le Miramar - a renowned seafood restaurant by the port—try the grilled lobster served with garlic butter.
- Enjoy a walk along the harbor at sunset.

Day 2: Cultural & Scenic Introduction to Marseille

Morning:

- MuCEM (Museum of European and Mediterranean Civilizations) – A perfect introduction to Marseille's history and architecture.
- Walk across Fort Saint-Jean for stunning Old Port views.

Afternoon:

- Lunch at Les Halles de la Major – A lively food hall where you can grab a quick and delicious meal like panisse (chickpea fries), sandwiches, or fresh seafood.
- Explore Le Panier, Marseille's oldest district, with colorful streets, local art, and charming cafés.
- Visit the Cathédrale de la Major for impressive architecture and harbor views.

Evening:

- Scenic walk along the Corniche Kennedy, stopping at Vallon des Auffes for sunset.
- Dinner at Le Petit Nice Passedat – A Michelin-starred experience featuring seafood and breathtaking sea views. Try the Bouillabaisse (Traditional Fish Stew).

Day 3: Adventure & Nature - Calanques & Paragliding

Morning:

- Head to Calanques National Park for an easy hike from Cassis to Calanque d'En-Vau.
- Swim in the turquoise waters and enjoy the breathtaking cliffs.

Afternoon:

- Lunch at Maison Casalini – A great grab-and-go pizza spot in Cassis, perfect for a quick but tasty meal before your next adventure.
- Paragliding over the Calanques – Soar above the dramatic cliffs and Mediterranean waters.

Evening:

- Dinner at La Table de l'Olivier – A gastronomic Mediterranean dining experience with creative flair. you may want to try the Seafood Risotto: Creamy risotto with mussels, shrimp, and calamari.
- Leisurely walk around the Old Port, enjoying the lively atmosphere.

Day 4: Boat Trip & Adventure Hike/Rock Climbing

Morning:

- Boat trip along the Mediterranean coast – Explore Frioul Islands, Château d'If, and hidden coves.

Afternoon:

- Lunch at a Boulangerie (Bakery) like Patisserie Amandine – Grab a fresh baguette sandwich, quiche, or a pissaladière (Provençal flatbread) for a quick and affordable meal.
- Adventurous hike or rock climbing in Les Goudes or Sugiton, offering stunning sea views.

Evening:

- Dinner at Chez Fonfon – A classic spot in Vallon des Auffes, known for Pan-Seared Sea Bass: Perfectly seared Mediterranean sea bass with a side of roasted vegetables.
- Drinks at a beach bar, such as La Rhumerie.

Day 5: Cycling, Rollerblading & Parc Borély

Morning:

- Cycling or rollerblading along Corniche Kennedy toward Parc Borély.
- Stroll through the park's beautiful gardens and fountains.

Afternoon:

- Lunch at Café Borély – A relaxed meal in the park with fresh, seasonal ingredients.
- Visit Basilique Notre-Dame de la Garde for the best panoramic views of Marseille.

Evening:

- Dinner at L'Épuisette – A seafood restaurant perched above the sea with a romantic sunset view and a focus on Mediterranean flavors. You may enjoy the Seafood Platter: A selection of fresh oysters, shrimp, mussels, and other Mediterranean seafood.
- Final scenic walk through the Saint-Victor district, stopping at a local wine bar.

Conclusion

Marseille offers unforgettable experiences for travelers, from scenic hikes to luxury dining and relaxing on the beaches. With plenty of outdoor activities, cultural experiences, and picturesque landscapes, Marseille presents something for every kind of traveler, whether you seek adventure, relaxation, or cultural immersion.

This guide is designed to help you plan your trip and make the most of your time in this amazing destination. If you find this book helpful, I would greatly appreciate it if you could leave a positive review on Amazon. Thank you!

Wishing you safe and enjoyable travels!

Resources

Airbnb. (n.d.). *Stays in Marseille, France.* Retrieved February 27, 2025, from https://www.airbnb.com/marseille-france/stays?utm_source=chatgpt.com

Aix-en-Provence Tourism. (n.d.). *Aix-en-Provence tourism: Official guide.* Aix-en-Provence Tourism. Retrieved February 27, 2025, from https://www.aixenprovencetourism.com

AllTrails. (n.d.). *AllTrails: Hiking, running, and biking trails.* AllTrails. Retrieved February 27, 2025, from https://www.alltrails.com

Aventure Alpes. (n.d.). *Guided rock climbing tours in the Calanques.* Retrieved February 27, 2025, from https://www.aventure-alpes.com

Booking.com. (n.d.). *Hotels, flights, car rentals, and more.* Booking.com. Retrieved February 27, 2025, from https://www.booking.com

Bureau des Guides de Marseille. (n.d.). *Paragliding in Marseille.* Retrieved February 27, 2025, from https://www.guides-marseille.com

Calanques National Park. (n.d.). *Rock climbing in the Calanques.* Retrieved February 27, 2025, from https://www.calanques-parcnati

onal.fr/en/discover/activities/rock-climbing

Carrefour. (n.d.). *Carrefour: Online shopping and groceries*. Carrefour. Retrieved February 27, 2025, from https://www.carrefour.fr

Expedia. (n.d.). *Flights from St. Louis to Marseille*. Retrieved February 27, 2025, from https://www.expedia.com/lp/flights/stl/mrs/st-louis-to-marseille

Intermarché. (n.d.). *Intermarché: Online shopping and groceries*. Intermarché. Retrieved February 27, 2025, from https://www.intermarche.com

Marseille Tourisme. (n.d.). *Marseille tourism: Official guide*. Marseille Tourisme. Retrieved February 27, 2025, from https://www.marseille-tourisme.com

Michelin. (n.d.). *Michelin guide: Restaurants and hotels*. Michelin. Retrieved February 27, 2025, from https://guide.michelin.com

MUCEM. (n.d.). *MUCEM: Museum of European and Mediterranean Civilizations*. MUCEM. Retrieved February 27, 2025, from https://www.mucem.org

Parc des Calanques. (n.d.). *Le Parc National des Calanques*. Parc des Calanques. Retrieved February 27, 2025, from https://www.parcdescalanques.fr

Pexels. (n.d.). *Pexels – Free stock photos & videos*. Pexels. Retrieved February 27, 2025, from https://www.pexels.com

RESOURCES

Provence Alpes Côte d'Azur. (n.d.). *Kayak and Stand-up Paddle in the Calanques*. Retrieved February 27, 2025, from https://www.provence-alpes-cotedazur.com

Skyscanner. (n.d.). *Flights from St. Louis to Marseille*. Retrieved February 27, 2025, from https://www.skyscanner.com/routes/stl/mrs/st-louis-to-marseille.html

Tripadvisor. (n.d.). *Tripadvisor: Read reviews, compare prices, and book*. Tripadvisor. Retrieved February 27, 2025, from https://www.tripadvisor.com

XE. (n.d.). *XE currency converter*. XE. Retrieved February 27, 2025, from https://www.xe.com

Printed in Dunstable, United Kingdom

66027652R00047